W9-CNZ-811

BOOKS BY ROBERT PENN WARREN

John Brown: The Making of a Martyr
Thirty-six Poems
Night Rider
Eleven Poems on the Same Theme
At Heaven's Gate
Selected Poems, 1923–1943
All the King's Men
Blackberry Winter
The Circus in the Attic
World Enough and Time
Brother to Dragons
Band of Angels
Segregation: The Inner Conflict in the South
Promises: Poems 1954–1956
Selected Essays
The Cave
All the King's Men (play)
You, Emperors, and Others: Poems 1957–1960
The Legacy of the Civil War
Wilderness
Flood
Who Speaks for the Negro?
Selected Poems: New and Old, 1923–1966
Incarnations: Poems 1966–1968
Audubon: A Vision
Homage to Theodore Dreiser
Meet Me in the Green Glen
Or Else—Poem/Poems 1968–1974
Democracy and Poetry
Selected Poems: 1923–1975
A Place to Come To
Now and Then: Poems 1976–1978
Brother to Dragons: A New Version
Being Here: Poetry 1977–1980

BEING HERE

Poetry 1977-1980

Robert
Penn Warren

BEING HERE

Poetry 1977-1980

Random House
New York

 Published in the United States by Random House, Inc., New York, and simultaneously in Canada by Random House of Canada Limited, Toronto.

Some of these poems originally appeared in *The American Poetry Review, Antaeus, The Atlantic Monthly, The Georgia Review, New England Review, The New York Review of Books, Poetry, Salmagundi, The Southern Review, Vanderbilt Poetry Review, The Washington Post (Book World), The Yale Review.*

The following poems appeared originally in *The New Yorker:* "Acquaintance with Time in Early Autumn," "August Moon," "Auto-da-Fé," "The Cross," "Preternaturally Early Snowfall in Mating Season," "Sky," and "Speleology."

Library of Congress Cataloging in Publication Data

Warren, Robert Penn, 1905–
Being here

I. Title.
PS3545.A748B4 1980 811'.52 80-11520
ISBN 0-394-51304-5
ISBN 0-394-73935-3 (pbk.)

Manufactured in the United States of America

9 8 7 6 5 4 3 2

To

GABRIEL THOMAS PENN
(1836–1920)

OLD MAN: You get old and you can't do anybody any good any more.

BOY: You do me some good, Grandpa. You tell me things.

There is in short no absolute time standard.

Van Nostrand's Scientific Encyclopedia,
Fifth Edition, p. 2203

I thirst to know the power and nature of Time . . .

St. Augustine: *Confessions,*
Book xi, Chapter 23
(translated by Albert C. Outler)

Time is the dimension in which God strives
to define His own Being.

CONTENTS

BEING HERE

Poetry 1977-1980

* This symbol is used to indicate a space between sections of a poem wherever such spaces are lost in pagination.

OCTOBER PICNIC LONG AGO

"Yassuh, here 'tis," Bumbo said, handing reins to the mister.
Fixed hampers and blankets behind and strapped them tight.
To the surrey helped Mother up, passed the baby to her,
While I, toward seven, kept my sister aright,
And over us all, in a flood, poured the golden October light.

Out of town, clop-clop, *till we found a side-lane that led*
Into woods, where gold leaves flicked a fairy shadow and light
That changed the known shape of a nose or face or head
Till we looked like a passel of circus freaks crammed tight
On four wheels, while the flickering nag was steered by a witch's sleight.

To a stream we came, and well tossed by stones, made crossing.
And there it was—as we might have known Father'd known:
A grass circle, and off to one side, by a boulder, a spring,
All ready for us, and a crude fireplace of stone.
Then quick as a wink, horse unhitched and staked, the big children gone.

All predictable, sure—a Sunday picnic like any
Of that old time when a stable rented an outfit,
That being before the auto had come, or many.
My mother's skirt was blue serge, long and close-fit.
My father's suede shoes were buttoned up high, and a Norfolk jacket.

All predictable—lunch, the baby asleep, children gone
But not far, and Father and Mother gone, hand in hand,
Heads together as though in one long conversation
That even now I can't think has had an end—
But where? Perhaps in some high, cloud-floating, and sunlit land.

But picnics have ends, and just as the sun set,
My mother cried out, "Could a place so beautiful be!"
And my father said, "My ship will come in yet,
And you'll see all the beautiful world there is to see."
"What more would I want," she now cried, "when I love everything I now see?"
*

So she swung the baby against the rose-tinted sky,
And a bird-note burst from her throat, and she gaily sang
As we clop-clopped *homeward while the shadows, sly,*
Leashed the Future up, like a hound with a slavering fang.
But sleepy, I didn't know what a Future was, as she sang.

And she sang.

I

SPELEOLOGY

At cliff-foot where great ledges thrust, the cave
Debouches, soil level and rank, where the stream,
Ages back, had come boiling forth, and now from alluvial earth
The last of old virgin forest trees rise to cliff-height,
And at noon twilight reigns. No one comes.

I must have been six when I first found the cave-mouth
Under ledges moss-green, and moss-green the inner dark.
Each summer I came, in twilight peered in, crept further,
Till one summer all I could see was a gray
Blotch of light far behind. Ran back. Didn't want to be dead.

By twelve, I was bolder. Besides, now had me a flashlight.
The whole night before couldn't sleep. Daylight. Then breakfast.
The cave wandered on, roof lower and lower except
Where chambers of darkness rose and stalactites down-stabbed
To the heart of my light. Again, lower.

I cut off the light. Knew darkness and depth and no Time.
Felt the cave-cricket crawl up an arm. Switched light on
To see the lone life there, the cave-cricket pale
As a ghost on my brown arm. I thought: *They are blind.*
Crept on. Heard, faintly, below

A silken and whispering rustle. Like what? Like water—so swung
The light to one side. I had crawled out
A ledge under which, far down, far down, the water yet channeled
And sang to itself, and answered my high light with swollen
White bursts of bubble. Light out, unmoving, I lay,

Lulled as by song in a dream, knowing
I dared not move in a darkness so absolute.
I thought: *This is me.* Thought: *Me—who am I?* Felt
Heart beating as though to a pulse of darkness and earth, and thought
How would it be to be here forever, my heart,
*

In its beat, part of all. Part of all—
But I woke with a scream. The flashlight,
It slipped, but I grabbed it. Had light—
And once more looked down the deep slicing and sluicing
Of limestone where water winked, bubbles like fish-eyes, a song like terror.

Years later, past dreams, I have lain
In darkness and heard the depth of that unending song,
And hand laid to heart, have once again thought: *This is me.*
And thought: *Who am I?* And hand on heart, wondered
What would it be like to be, in the end, part of all.

And in darkness have even asked: *Is this all? What is all?*

WHEN LIFE BEGINS

Erect was the old Hellenistic head,
White-thatched in that dark cedar shade,
Curl-tangled the beard like skill-carved stone
With chisel-grooved shadow accenting the white.
The blue gaze fixed on a mythic distance.

That distance, a far hill's horizon, bulged
Past woods into the throbbing blue
Of a summer's afternoon. The silence
There seemed to have substantial life
That was the death of the pulse of Time.

One hand, gnarled, liver-blotched, but sinewed
From wrestling with the sleight of years,
Lay propped on a blue-jeaned knee and wrapped
Around a cob pipe, from which one thread
Of smoke, more blue than distance, rose
To twine into the cedar-dark.

The boy—he felt he wasn't there.
He felt that all reality
Had been cupboarded in that high head,
But now was absorbed into the abstractness
Of that blue gaze, so fixed and far,
Aimed lethally past the horizon's fact.

He thought all things that ever lived
Had gone to live behind that brow,
And in their infinite smallness slept
Until the old voice might wake them again
To strive in the past but passionate

Endeavor—hoofbeat at night, steel-clang,
Boom of the battery to take,
Far smoke seen long before you hear sound,

And before that, too, the gust of grape
Overhead, through oak leaves. Your stallion rears.

Your stallion rears—yes, it is you!

With your glasses you spot, from east, from west,
From woods-cover, skirmishers mincing out
On both flanks of that rise. Rifle-fire
Prickles the distance, noiseless, white.
Then a shell bursts over that fanged, far hill,
Single, annunciatory, like
A day-star over new Bethlehem.

In the country-quiet, momentarily
After that event renewed, one lone
Quail calls.

And the old man, once he said
How a young boy, dying, broke into tears.
"Ain't scairt to die"—the boy's words—"it's jist
I ne'er had no chance to know what tail's like."

Hunger and thirst, and the quavering yell
That more than bugle gave guts to a charge,
And once said: "My Mary, her hands were like silk,
But strong—and her mount on his shadow would dance."
Once said: "But things—they can seem like a dream."

Old eyelids shut the horizon out.
The boy sat and wondered when life would begin,
Nor knew that, beyond the horizon's heave,
Time crouched, like a great cat, motionless
But for tail's twitch. Night comes. Eyes glare.

BOYHOOD IN TOBACCO COUNTRY

All I can dream tonight is an autumn sunset,
Red as a hayrick burning. The groves,
Not yet leafless, are black against red, as though,
Leaf by leaf, they were hammered of bronze blackened
To timelessness. Far off, from the curing barns of tobacco,
Blue smoke, in pale streaking, clings
To the world's dim, undefinable bulge.

Far past slashed stubs, homeward or homeless, a black
Voice, deeper and bluer than sea-heart, sweeter
Than sadness or sorghum, utters the namelessness
Of life to the birth of a first star,
And again, I am walking a dust-silent, dusky lane, and try
To forget my own name and be part of the world.

I move in its timelessness. From the deep and premature midnight
Of woodland, I hear the first whip-o-will's
Precious grief, and my young heart,
As darkling I stand, yearns for a grief
To be worthy of that sound. Ah, fool! Meanwhile,
Arrogant, eastward, lifts the slow dawn of the harvest moon.

Enormous, smoky, smoldering, it stirs.
First visibly, then paling in retardation, it begins
The long climb zenithward to preside
There whitely on what the year has wrought.
What have the years wrought? I walk the house.
Oh, grief! Oh, joy! Tonight
The same season's moon holds sky-height.

The dark roof hides the sky.

FILLING NIGHT WITH THE NAME: FUNERAL AS LOCAL COLOR

It was all predictable, and just as well.
For old Mrs. Clinch at last lay gut-rigid there
In the coffin, withered cheeks subtly rouged, hair
Frizzled and tinted, with other marks of skill
Of the undertaker to ready his client to meet
Her God and her grave-worm—well, Mrs. Clinch had heard
The same virtues extolled for the likes of her, word for word,
With no word, true or false, that she couldn't exactly repeat.

In piety, a friendly old couple offered
To see Mr. Clinch through the night, cook supper and breakfast.
"When a thing's gonna be," he replied, "git used to it fast."
Thanked them all. Remarked on the grave now flower-coffered.
Shook the preacher's hand. Wiped the tear from a wind-blue eye.
Dropped off at his farm. Not hungry, no supper. Near sundown,
Good clothes still on, went to milk. His forehead pressed down
On the cow's coarse hide. At last, milk ran tinnily.

Milk on ice, he climbed out of Sunday blue serge, and right
Where the box-toed black shoes got set, he hung it above.
Bed pulled back, he stared at the infinite tundra of
Starched sheets by some kindly anonymous hand pulled tight.
He couldn't crawl in. It seemed all was happening still.
So got pen, paper, ink. Sat down to write to his boy,
Far away. But no word would come, and sorrow and joy
All seemed one—just the single, simple word *whip-o-will.*

For the bird was filling the night with the name: *whip-o-will.*

Whip-o-will.

RECOLLECTION IN UPPER ONTARIO, FROM LONG BEFORE

(for Richard Eberhart)

Why do I still wake up and not know?—though later
By years, and a thousand miles north, on the Hudson Bay slope,
Lost in forests and lakes, while the embers
In evergreen darkness die, and just
Beyond the black lace of low bough-droop
Sky shows, and stars sown random and rabble and white. The loon
Bursts out laughing again at his worn-out
Joke, and I wonder if it is on me.
That is, if mine could be called one.

Anyway, one kind of a joke is on me, for
There's no locomotive in three hundred miles—and sure,
No express, no old-fashioned, brass-bound eight-wheeler,
To wake up the loon to maniacal stitches.
And if the great owl calls, I know
It can't be because of a locomotive, none near.

When the last ember winks, and the dark,
Crawling near, now means business, and I
Am asleep, then again
The express, now bound hell-for-leather in dream,
The cylinders spewing white steam, comes boiling
Over the hill. Will it come? Really get here, this time?

I don't know for sure. The owl—
He may wake me again
With his same old gargle of question,
The question he ought long back to have answered,
But asks just for fun.
Or to make your conscience ask if it's you who—*who-who*—
Did whatever it was.

But no owl speaks yet, no loon. I sleep on. And again
Old Zack, pore ole white-trash—croker sack dragging—
Is out to scrounge coal off the L & N tracks.

Old Mag at it too, face knobby, eyes bleared,
Mouth dribbling with snuff, skirts swinging
Above the old brogan she's fixed for her clubfoot,
And dragging her own sack for coal.
They don't hear the whistle. Or Zack's
Just stubborn, born democrat, knowing damned well
That the coal, it is his, and by rights.
Then the whistle again, in outrage and anguish.

And now I wake up, or not. If I don't
It blows on like hell, brakes screaming,
And Mag, of a sudden, is down. The brogan she wears
For the clubfoot, it looks like it's caught
In a switch-*V*—the coal chute starts here.
And I stand in a weedy ditch, my butterfly
Net in my hand, my chloroform jar,
Mount box, and canteen strung on me—and Zack,
He keeps pulling. She's up. Zack bends at the brogan.
The whistle goes wild. Brakes scream. I stare.

Zack's up, foot's out! Or is it? A second she's standing,
Then down—now over both rails—
Down for good, and the last
Thing I see is his hands out. To grab her, I reckoned.

Time stops like it's no-Time. Then,
The express, I see it back up. The porters, conductors,
With bed sheets, pile out. I see
The first sheet pass. It sags. It drips. So
Out ditch and over, I'm gone. Look back once
When autos, the sheriff and coroner, come. I look
In my jar: the Gulf State fritillary quiet as a leaf,
Black and gold. Near dark by this time.
I make home, remembering the porter
Who said: "Hell—it's hamburger now!"

I wonder what's coming for supper.

"An accident"—that's what the coroner said, and no tale
For the news-sheet, except a collection

To bury Old Mag. Few came in the rain.
Then on Saturday night, on the street,
It's Zack, now drunk as a coot. He grabs me, he says—
Says: "Yeah, you come spyen on me!
Down thar in the ditch, in them weeds. Well, you're wrong!"

His face, its likker-breath hot on my face—it says:
"I ne'er tetched her! She fell. Nigh got myself kilt
Count of her durn shoe!" Then he,
Old fingers like rusty nails in my biceps: "Stuck up!
You durn little butterfly ketcher—but got enough sense
To haul-ass afore the durn coroner come." So shoved me.

Was gone. And I stood in the crowd of a Saturday night
On a market-town street, years ago,
When farm-folks and tenants, they came in to trade.
I stood there. And something inside me, it grew.

And that night in bed, like a dream but not one, I saw.
Saw inside of Zack's ruin of a shack, and a coal-oil
Lamp flickered, and Zack and his Mag, young now,
Getting ready for bed, them maybe just married.
Saw how she was trying to get off her gear and not show
That foot. Yes, there in my head, I saw it, and saw
How he took it, the foot. Leaned over and kissed it.

And tears gone bright in her eyes.

But all the years later I'd only see
How he'd try not to see it. Then
Blow out the lamp. And if summer,
He'd stare up in darkness. If winter,
And fire on the hearth, lie watching
The shadows dance on the ceiling. And handle himself.
To make himself grab her.

But now, far north, I'm asleep and deep
In the old real dream: the brass-bound express
Comes boiling over the hill, whistle crazy—but that's

Far north, in the woods, and the loon
Begins laughing his crazy fool head off. To wake me.

Stars paled. That was all.

Dawn burst in a riot of glory: chips on the cook-fire,
Smell of bacon, camp struck, canoes waiting easy and yearning.
We glide out, mine first, on the unrippling sheen
Of day's silver and gold, and the paddle dips to a rhythm
That feels like the world's own breath, and behind us
A voice is singing its joy—and is this
The same world I stood in,
In the ditch, years ago,
And saw what I saw?

Or what did I see?

THE MOONLIGHT'S DREAM

Why did I wake that night, all the house at rest?
I could not hear, but knew what each breath meant
In each room. My father's long drag to the depth of his chest.
My mother's like silk or the rustle of lilies that leant
By the garden pool when night breeze was merely a whisper.
But loudest of all, that of my old grandfather,
Who with years now struggled, grumbling, croupy, and slow,
But one night had roused to a blood-yell, dreaming Fort Pillow or Shiloh.

Tonight the house was mouse-still except for some beam
That, whisper or creak, complained of the years it had borne
The weight of reality and the human dream
As the real became more real, and the real more forlorn.
Outside, I wondered why I had come out and where
I would go, and back-looking, now saw the tracks of my bare
Dark footprints set in the moonlit dew like snow,
And thought: *I go where they go, for they must know where we go.*

It was as though they did know the way in a dream
The moonlight was having of all the world that night,
And they followed the path that wandered down to a stream
Where cattle snorted in shadow, their eyes without sight
Staring through the dream that I was, while a whip-o-will
Asserted to moonlight its name, while nameless and still,
I wondered if ever my heart would beat again,
As I wandered the moonlight's dream, past pleasure or past pain.

Across the sweet-clover whiteness, then up the hill
To the darkness that hung from old maples, and lay down to wonder
If I, being part of the moonlight's dream, could be real,
For whatever realness I was, it must lie asleep yonder
In the far, white house that was part of the moonlight's dream, too.
Then blankness. At day-streak, in terror, I woke, ran through
The tangle of clover, corn-balk, the creek, home to bed:
But no breath could I hear, for all seemed still, as still as the dead.
*

Not dead! Though long years now are, and the creek bulldozed dry,
And their sorrow and joy, their passion and pain and endeavor,
Have with them gone, with whatever reality
They were, or are, by sunlight or moonlight—whatever.
The highway has slicked the spot the white farmhouse once stood.
At sixty per I am whirled past the spot where my blood
Is unwitting of that as of the defunct stream,
Or of the ignorant night I strayed in the moonlight's dream.

THE ONLY POEM

The only poem to write I now have in mind
May not be written because of memory, or eyes.
The scene is too vivid, so tears, not words, I may find.
If perhaps I forget, it might catch me by surprise.

The facts lie long back, and surely are trivial,
Though I've waked in the night, as though at a voice at my ear,
Till a flash of the dying dream comes back, and I haul
Up a sheet-edge to angrily wipe at an angry tear.

My mother was middle-aged, and then retained
Only sweetness of face, not the beauty my father, years later,
Near death, would try to describe, but words blurring, refrained.
But the facts: that day she took me to see the new daughter

My friends stashed with Grandma while they went East for careers.
So for friendship I warily handled the sweet-smelling squaw-fruit,
All golden and pink, kissed the fingers, blew in the ears.
Then suddenly was at a loss. So my mother seized it,

And I knew, all at once, that she would have waited all day,
Sitting there on the floor, with her feet drawn up like a girl,
Till half-laughing, half-crying, arms stretched, she could swing up her prey
That shrieked with joy at the giddy swoop and swirl.

Yes, that was all, except for the formal farewell,
And wordless we wandered the snow-dabbled street, and day,
With her hands both clutching my arm till I thought it would swell.
Then home, fumbling key, she said: "Shucks! Time gets away."

We entered. She laid out my supper. My train left at eight
To go back to the world where all is always the same.
Success or failure—what can alleviate
The pang of unworthiness built into Time's own name?

PLATONIC DROWSE

The shaft of paralyzed sunlight.
White cat by the rose bush crouching
Beneath the last blowzy red

Of the season, its eyes, slow
Blinking. Sun-glint gold on
The brown of enameled wasps weaving

Around one gold pear, high-hung.
It is far beyond your reach.
A rooster crows, far, thin.

The sun is nailed to the sky
To bless forever that land
Where only Time dies.

You do not think this is true.
You laugh. Fool, don't you remember?
You lay in the browning, tall

Grass, in unaimed pubescent
Grief, but the grief, it
Shriveled to nothing. Oh, lost!

But your body began to flow
On every side into distance,
Unrippling, silent, silver,

Leaving only the steady but pulsing
Germ-flame of your Being, that throbbed
In Platonic joy for the world.

The world, in Platonic drowse, lay.

GRACKLES, GOODBYE

Black of grackles glints purple as, wheeling in sun-glare,
The flock splays away to pepper the blueness of distance.
Soon they are lost in the tracklessness of air.
I watch them go. I stand in my trance.

Another year gone. In trance of realization,
I remember once seeing a first fall leaf, flame-red, release
Bough-grip, and seek, through gold light of the season's sun,
Black gloss of a mountain pool, and there drift in peace.

Another year gone. And once my mother's hand
Held mine while I kicked the piled yellow leaves on the lawn
And laughed, not knowing some yellow-leaf season I'd stand
And see the hole filled. How they spread their obscene fake lawn.

Who needs the undertaker's sick lie
Flung thus in the teeth of Time, and the earth's spin and tilt.
What kind of fool would promote that kind of lie?
Even sunrise and sunset convict the half-wit of guilt.

Grackles, goodbye! The sky will be vacant and lonely
Till again I hear your horde's rusty creak high above,
Confirming the year's turn and the fact that only, only,
In the name of Death do we learn the true name of Love.

II

YOUTHFUL TRUTH-SEEKER, HALF-NAKED, AT NIGHT, RUNNING DOWN BEACH SOUTH OF SAN FRANCISCO

In dark, climbing up. Then down-riding the sand sluice
Beachward from dune-head. Running, feet bare on
Sand wet-packed and star-stung. Phlegm in lungs loose.
Though now tide turning, spume yet prickling air on

My chest, which naked, splits darkness. On the right hand,
Palisades of white-crashing breakers renew and stretch on
Into unmooned drama and distance.—To understand
Is impossible now. Flight from what? To what? And alone.

Far behind, the glow of the city of men fades slow.
And ahead, white surf and dark dunes in dimness are wed,
While Pacificward, leagues afar, fog threatens to grow,
But on I yet run, face up, stars shining above my wet head

Before they are swaddled in grayness, though grayness, perhaps,
Is what waits—after history, logic, philosophy too,
Even rhythm of lines that bring tears to the heart, and scraps
Of old wisdom that like broken bottles in darkness gleam at you.

What was the world I had lived in? Poetry, orgasm, joke:
And the joke the biggest on me, the laughing despair
Of a truth the heart might speak, but never spoke—
Like the twilit whisper of wings with no shadow on air.

You dream that somewhere, somehow, you may embrace
The world in its fullness and threat, and feel, like Jacob, at last
The merciless grasp of unwordable grace
Which has no truth to tell of future or past—

But only life's instancy, by daylight or night,
While constellations strive, or a warbler whets
His note, or the ice creaks blue in white-night Arctic light,
Or the maniac weeps—over what he always forgets.
*

So lungs aflame now, sand raw between toes,
And the city grows dim, dimmer still,
And the grind of breath and of sand is all one knows
Of the Truth a man flees to, or from, in his angry need to fulfill

What?—On the beach flat I fall by the foam-frayed sea
That now and then brushes an outflung hand, as though
In tentative comfort, yet knowing itself to be
As ignorant as I, and as feckless also.

So I stare at the stars that remain, shut eyes, in dark press an ear
To sand, cold as cement, to apprehend,
Not merely the grinding of shingle and sea-slosh near,
But the groaning miles of depth where light finds its end.

Below all silken soil-slip, all crinkled earth-crust,
Far deeper than ocean, past rock that against rock grieves,
There at the globe's deepest dark and visceral lust,
Can I hear the *groan-swish* of magma that churns and heaves?

No word? No sign? Or is there a time and place—
Ice-peak or heat-simmered distance—where heart, like eye,
May open? But sleep at last—it has sealed up my face,
And last foam, retreating, creeps from my hand. It will dry,

While fog, star by star, imperially claims the night.
How long till dawn flushes dune-tops, or gilds beach-stones?
I stand up. Stand thinking, I'm one poor damn fool, all right.
Then ask, if years later, I'll drive again forth under stars, on tottering bones.

SNOWSHOEING BACK TO CAMP IN GLOAMING

Scraggle and brush broken through, snow-shower jarred loose
To drape shoulders, dead boughs, snow-sly and trap-laid,
Snatching thongs of my snowshoes, I
Stopped. At the edge of the high mountain mowing,
I stood. Westward stared
At the half mile of white alabaster unblemished
To the blackness of spruce forest lifting
In a long scree-climb to cliff-thrust,
Where snow, in level striation of ledges, stretched, and the sun,
Unmoving, hung
Clear yet of the peak-snagged horizon—
The sun, by a spectral spectrum belted,
Pale in its ghost-nimb.

The shadow of spruces, magenta,
Bled at me in motionlessness
Across unmarred white of the mowing.

Time died in my heart.

So I stood on that knife-edge frontier
Of Timelessness, knowing that yonder
Ahead was the life I might live
Could I but move
Into the terror of unmarred whiteness under
The be-nimbed and frozen sun.

While behind, I knew,
In the garrote of perfect knowledge, that
The past flowed backward: trees bare
As though of all deeds unleafed, and
Dead leaves lost are only
Old words forgotten in snowdrifts.
*

But the crow in distance called, and I knew
He spoke truth, for

Higher a wash of pale pink suddenly tinted the mowing,
And from spruce-blackness magenta
Leaped closer. But at
That instant, sun-nimb
Made contact with jag-heave of mountain.
Magenta lapped suddenly gray at my feet,
With pink, farther up,
Going gray.

Hillward and sky-thrust, behind me,
Leafless and distanced to eastward, a huge
Beech clung to its last lone twinge
Of pink on the elephant-gray—far under
One star.

Now the track, gone pale in tree-night,
Downward floated before me, to darkness,

So starward I stared
To the unnamed void where Space and God
Flinch to come, and where
Un-Time roars like a wind that only
The dead, unweeping, hear.

Oh, Pascal!
What does a man need to forget?

But moved on, however, remembering
That somewhere—somewhere, it seemed—
Beautiful faces above a hearthstone bent
Their inward to an outward glow.

Remembering, too, that when a door upon dark
Opens, and I, fur-prickled with frost,
Against the dark stand, one gaze
Will lift and smile with sudden sheen
Of a source far other than firelight—or even

Imagined star-glint.

WHY HAVE I WANDERED THE ASPHALT OF MIDNIGHT?

Why have I wandered the asphalt of midnight and not known why?
Not guilt, or joy, or expectation, or even to know how,
When clouds were tattered, the distance beyond screamed its rage,
Or when fog broke
To clarity—not even to know how the strict
Rearrangement of stars communicated
Their mystic message to
The attent corpuscles hurrying heartward, and from.

Why did I stand with no motion under
The spilt-ink darkness of spruces and try to hear,
In the soundlessness of falling snow,
The heartbeat I know as the only self
I know that I know, while History
Trails its meaning like old cobwebs
Caught in a cellar broom?

Why should I clamber the cliff now gone bone-white in moonlight?
Just to feel blood dry like a crust on hands, or watch
The moon lean westering to the next range,
The next, and beyond,
To wash the whole continent, like spume?
Why should I sit till from the next valley I hear
The great bear's autumnal sex-hoot
Or the glutted owl make utterance?

Why should I wander dark dunes till rollers
Boom in from China, stagger, and break
On the beach in frothed mania, while high to the right
The North Star holds steady enough to be Truth?

Yes, why, all the years, and places, and nights, have I
Wandered and not known the question I carried?
And carry? Yes, sometimes, at dawn,
I have seen the first farmer

Set bright the steel share to the earth, or met,
Snowshoed, the trapper just set on his dawn-rounds.
Or even, long back, on a streetcar
Bound cityward, watched some old workman
Lean over his lunch box, and yawn.

AUGUST MOON

Gold like a half-slice of orange
Fished from a stiff Old-Fashioned, the moon
Lolls on the sky that goes deeper blue
By the tick of the watch. Or
Lolls like a real brass button half-buttoned
On the blue flannel sleeve
Of an expensive seagoing blue blazer.

Slowly stars, in a gradual
Eczema of glory, gain definition.

What kind of world is this we walk in?

It makes no sense except
The inner, near-soundless *chug-chug* of the body's old business—
Your father's cancer, or
Mother's stroke, or
The cat's fifth pregnancy.

Anyway, while night
Hardens into its infinite being,
We walk down the woods-lane, dreaming
There's an inward means of
Communication with
That world whose darkling susurration
Might—if only we were lucky—be
Deciphered.

Children do not count years
Except at birthday parties.
We count them unexpectedly,
At random, like
A half-wit pulling both triggers
Of a ten-gauge with no target, then
*

Wondering what made the noise,
Or what hit the shoulder with the flat
Butt of the axe-head.

But this is off the point, which is
The counting of years, and who
Wants to live anyway
Except to be of use to
Somebody loved?

At least, that's what they say.

Do you hear the great owl in distance?

Do you remember a childhood prayer—
A hand on your head?

The moon is lost in tree-darkness.
Stars show now only
In the pale path between treetops.
The track of white gravel leads forward in darkness.

I advise you to hold hands as you walk,
And speak not a word.

DREAMING IN DAYLIGHT

You clamber up rock, crash thicket, leap
Brook, stop for breath—then standing still, quote

A few lines of verse in the emptiness of silence. Then
Past birches, up bluffside—or near-cliff, it is. Breath

Again short, you crouch, feeling naked to think
That from crevice of stone, from shadow of leaf,

From rotted-out log, from earth-aperture,
Small eyes, or larger, with glitter in darkness, are watching

Your every move. They are like conscience. They are
Like remorse. You don't belong

Here, and that is why, like gastritis
Or migraine, something mysterious

Is going on inside you, but with no name. Do you
Know your own name? Do you feel that

You barely escape the last flicker of foam
Just behind, up the beach of

History—indeed, that you are
The last glint of consciousness before

You are caught by the grind, bulge, and beat of
What has been? Indeed, by

The heaving ocean of pastness? Oh, try
To think of something your life has meant,

While from darkness bright eyes fix now on your strangeness.
They do not know that you are stranger
*

To yourself than to them. Move higher!
For the past creeps behind you, like foam. At last

Rears the stern rock, majestic and snagged, that
The peak is. It thrusts from green growth. Is sky-bare.

You clamber the few mossed shards that frost has ripped off.
Then stop. For no handholds nub the raw pylon. This

Is the end. You think: *I am here.*
You expect to see foam, so white, so silent, snaking

Out from green brush. You wait. You think
That all you can do is to try to remember,

And name by name, aloud, the people you have
Truly loved. And you find that difficult. They are so few.

That night, in your bed, you wake from a dream
Of eyes that from crevice, shade, log, aperture,

Peer. They peer, dark-glistening, like
Conscience. Yes, you are less strange to them

Than to yourself.

PRETERNATURALLY EARLY SNOWFALL IN MATING SEASON

Three days back, first snow had fallen.
Light, no more than a sprinkling of sugar
Crystalline on brown hickory leaves
And gold-fading beech leaves fallen:
Just like the breakfast of champions. Upridge,
However, spruces were spangled. The sun,
With remote indifference, heatless,
Fulfilled its shortening arc
From ridge to far ridge in the mountains, grasping
Earth's globe in merciless fingers, the globe
Black-furred. I slept
With foot of sleeping sack near dying coals. Frontiersmen,
I'd read, learned early to beat the chronic curse
Of rheumatism: set wet moccasined feet—which, with wry wit
They said, was just a worse way of going barefoot—
Toward fire to sleep.

Skyward, no stars.

Morning, no sun, not even
One leprous wan wen of light; only
Grayness diffused under a dome
Like gray stone crudely set
In gray cement of prehistory,
The dome bulwarked to ride
The horizon's snagged circle. Clouds, like gray stone,
Bellied down: the real thing coming, and soon.

Early, but snowshoes in tote. Pure luck.

On such a day the mind, like sky,
Has no thought; only the sagging promise of itself.
Your mind hangs gray, like the dome of cloud-stone. Hands
Do their tasks, alone, unsupervised:
They are the single point of the world.
*

This is one name for happiness: the act.

Past midnight, snow on face, I woke.
Re-fed the fire. Crawled back in sack,
Drew tighter the hood, wondered
How is whiteness a darkness, and in that hypnosis,
Slept. Then started up at a blast, wheeze, snort, bleat,
And beat and crash of dead boughs. One moment,
Bewildered. Then knew.

In the world of glitter and dawn-snow whiteness,
My snowshoes at last being dug out, I found the spot.
First, where a doe, by a deadfall, had made her huddle. Then
Where the buck had wrestled and struggled to mount.
There were the poplar boughs, rotten, beat loose by the antlers.
There, scarcely covered by new snow, the marks
Of plunge, stamp, trample, heave, and ecstasy of storm.

It took two days, snowshoeing, to get out,
And rations short the second. My skull
Felt scraped inside as though scrubbed with ammonia,
And I moved through the white world, nothing
Inside the skull but the simple awareness of Being. But
Just once, toward dark, the white world gone gray,
I stopped for breath, and standing, was sure, with leap
Of heart, I was for an instant actually seeing,
Even in that gloom, directly before me, the guessed-at glory.

By that time I must have been pretty beat
From fatigue and hunger. And later
It was hard to get a fire going.

SILA

Sila, for the Eskimo, "is the air, not the sky; movement, not wind; the very breath of life, but not physical life; he is clear-sighted energy, activating intelligence; the powerful fluid circulating 'all around' and also within each individual . . ."
LAROUSSE WORLD MYTHOLOGY

Upgrade, past snow-tangled bramble, past
Deadfall snow-buried, there—
The ruin of old stonework, where man-heart
Long ago had once lifted
In joy, and back muscles strained. "Stay, Sila!" the boy
Commanded the tawny great husky, broad-chested,
That in harness yet stood, forward-leaning. The boy
Stamped his cross-countries. Stared
At the ruin. Thought:
Two hundred years back—and it might
Have been me.

And wondered what name the man
Might have had. Thought:
Well, summer, I'll come
And hunt for the gravestones. Then thought
How letters that crude must be weathered away—how deeper
A skull must be pulping to earth, and now grinless.
But thought: *At least, I can touch it, whatever*
It is, stone or skull.

Was young, then he thought, *young as me, maybe.*

Then felt muscles tighten and clinch
At a sudden impulse of surprise
To find here the old mark of life that for life
Once had sung, while the axe-edge glittered in sunlight.

Oh, what are the years! his heart cried, and he felt
His own muscles pulsing in joy, just as when
Hands clasp for the lift of the beauty of butt-swell.
*

Land benched here, great beeches,
Gray, leafless, arising parklike and artful
From snow artificial as Christmas.
"Stay, Sila!" he called, and on level ground now
Slick glided to where the blue gleam of ice-eyes
Looked up in his own, with a knowledge deeper than words.
He snapped harness loose, wrapped cords at his waist, and—
The dog exploded.

From behind a beech deadfall, the doe, it had leaped,
Cow-awkward on earth, but magically airy in flight,
And weightless as wind, forelegs airward prowing
To seem as frail as a spider's, but hooves aglitter like glass
To cleave sunlight. Then,
Suddenly knifing the ice-crust as deep
As a trap, while the husky's wide paw-spread
Had opened like snowshoes behind.
Five leaps—and first blood, at a haunch,
Flesh laid back like a hunter's thin knife-slice.

Again, two more leaps, and white slash at belly—
Red line drawn clean on the curve. The boy's order
No use now: "Stay! Damn it, stay!" Until
Hand on harness, at last and too late, for
Red blood dripped now from white fang
To whiteness of snow, and eyes blue as steel drove into
The boy's eyes brain-deep, while, that instant,
All eons of friendship fled.
Then dog-eyes went earthward. The guts
Of the doe slip forth blue on the ice-crust.

The husky, stiff as in bronze cast, waits.

Only one thing to do. Who'd leave the doe there,
Dying slow into sunset, while all the small teeth—
Fox, field mouse, and wildcat—emerge
For their nocturnal feast? So the boy's knees bend.
Break the snow-crust like prayer,
And he cuddles the doe's head, and widening brown eyes
Seem ready, almost, to forgive.
*

Throat fur is cream color, eyes flecked with gold glintings.
He longs for connection, to give explanation. Sudden,
The head, now helpless, drops back on his shoulder. Twin eyes
Hold his own entrapped in their depth,
But his free hand, as though unaware,
Slides slow back
To grope for the knife-sheath.

The boy could not shut his eyes to the task,
As some fool girl might, but set
Eyes deeper in eyes, as he cradled the head, and gently
Held up the soft chin
To tauten the fullness of throat, and then,
As scrupulous as a well-trained tailor, set
The knife's needle point where acuteness
Would enter without prick of pain, and
Slashed in a single, deep motion.

He was sure that the doe
Never twitched.

On snow unconsciously heaped, he let down the head,
Aware even yet of the last embracement of gaze.
He watched, bewitched by the beauty, how blood flowed,
Red petal by petal, a great rose that bloomed where he stood.
How petal on petal, curve swelling past curve,
Gleamed forth at his feet on the snow,
And each petal sparkled with flicker of ice through the crimson,
As rays of last sun found a special glory in smallness.

He lifted his head, knife yet in hand, and westward
Fixed eyes beyond beech-bench to the snow-hatched
Stone thrust of the mountain, above which sky, too,
More majestically bloomed, but petals paler as higher—
The rose of the blood of the day. Still as stone,
So he stood. Then slowly—so slowly—
He raised the blade of the knife he loved honing, and wiped
The sweet warmness and wetness across his own mouth,
And set tongue to the edge of the silk-whetted steel.
*

He knew he knew something at last
That he'd never before known.
No name for it—no!

He snow-cleaned the knife. Sheathed it. Called: "Come!"
The dog, now docile, obeyed. With bare hands full of snow,
The boy washed him of blood and, comblike,
With fingers ennobled the ruff.

Then suddenly clasping the creature, he,
Over raw fur, past beeches, the mountain's snow-snag,
And the sky's slow paling of petals,
Cried out into vastness
Of silence: "Oh, world!"

He felt like a fool when tears came.

Some sixty years later, propped on death's pillow,
Again will he see that same scene, and try,
Heart straining, to utter that cry?—But
Cannot, breath short.

III

EMPTY WHITE BLOTCH ON MAP OF UNIVERSE: A POSSIBLE VIEW

The world is that map's white blotch, no charted coast.
The world is a strange shore for shipwreck, the last of choices.
The world is a strange bed to wake in—lost, lost.
The world is an island, strange, full of faceless voices.
What a landfall the world!—on which to be naked cast
By the infinite wind-heave, and wind-shoveled sea, of a father's lust.

Though this island is full of voices, I've never seen
Who sings, or grasped in what language the lyrics are.
I have followed the voices through forests of lethal green,
But the sweeter the note, the note is more far—more far.
Though in dream I see, as I hear that note again,
The wet thigh of a nymph, by a spring, agleam where stars peer in.

In the loneliest places I've wandered. I've clambered, stood
On a ruined cairn raised by lost aboriginals
To honor their dead (but who honored the last?)—and a flood
Of old orations from school I pronounced to the squalls
Of gulls and tern-laughter, as though they understood
My comic charade thus venting youth's view of the noble and good.

And I saw the very delusions before my sight:
Bloody Spartacus or the hair-combing Spartan few,
Or the neat little captain who'd not begun to fight,
Or at Gettysburg, old, angular Abe eschew
The rhetorical ordure which is the patriot's delight.
Oh, yes, I saw them—then all went black, of a sudden, as night.

I have written whole books, with a stone-honed reed on the sand,
Telling truth that should never be told, and what such truths mean.
But who cared? For Truth must accept its reprimand
When the tide comes in like Christ's blood, to wash all clean,
Including the truth that Truth's only a shout, or clapped hand,
At the steel-heeled stomp, steel-throated bark, or a lifted wand.
*

I have even erected a cross, looped my wrists, hung suspended—
There being no Roman ready with nails for the feet
Or to pierce my side with a spear—as God intended.
As for sponge and vinegar, neither—all incomplete.
But *"lama sabachthani,"* I cried. And attended
The premature dark, the shudder of earth, how all would be ended.

But no, no such end. On the blazing tropic sky
The vulture cruised, nor gave me the slightest attention.
At night, wriggling down, I bathed wrists, and crept to lie
In my cave, with no prayer, and no hope of change of condition.
But dreamed, while the surf kept beating its monody,
Of voices beguiling the distance—like pain, their love-stung cry.

FUNCTION OF BLIZZARD

God's goose, neck neatly wrung, is being plucked.
And night is blacker for the plethora
Of white feathers except when, in an air-tower beam,
Black feathers turn white as snow. Which is what they are.
And in the blind trajectory travelers scream toward silence.

Black ruins of arson in the Bronx are whitely
Redeemed. Poverty does not necessarily
Mean unhappiness. Can't you hear the creak of bed-slats
Or ghostly echo of childish laughter? Bless
Needle plunging into pinched vein. Bless coverings-over, forgettings.

Bless snow, and chains beating undersides of fenders.
Bless insane sirens of the Fire Department
And Christmas whirl of alarm lights. Bless even
Three infants locked in a tenement in Harlem.
God's bosom is broad. Snow soon will cover the anguished ruin.

Bless snow! Bless God, Who must work under the hand of
Fate, who has no name. God does the best
He can, and sometimes lets snow whiten the world
As a promise—as now of mystic comfort to
The old physicist, a Jew, faith long since dead, who is getting

High-lonesome drunk by the frosted window of
The Oak Room bar in the Plaza. And bless me, even
With no glass in my hand, and far from New York, as I rise
From bed, feet bare, heart freezing, to stare out at
The whitening fields and forest, and wonder what

Item of the past I'd most like God to let
Snow fall on, keep falling on, and never

Melt, for I, like you, am only a man, after all.

DREAM, DUMP-HEAP, AND CIVILIZATION

Like the stench and smudge of the old dump-heap
Of Norwalk, Connecticut, the residue

Of my dream remains, but I make no
Sense of even the fragments. They are nothing

More significant than busted iceboxes and stinking mattresses
Of Norwalk, and other such human trash from which

Smudge rose by day, or coals winked red by night,
Like a sign to the desert-walkers

Blessed by God's promise. Keep your foot on the gas,
And you'll get to Westport. But

What of my dream—stench, smudge, and fragments?
And behind it all a morning shadow, like guilt, strives.

To say what? How once I had lied to my mother and hid
In a closet and said, in darkness, aloud: "I hate you"?

Or how once, in total fascination, I watched a black boy
Take a corn knife and decapitate six kittens? Did I dream

That again last night? How he said: "Too many, dem"?
Did I dream of six kitten-heads staring all night at me?

All try to say something—still now trying
By daylight? Their blood inexhaustibly drips. Did I wake

With guilt? How rarely is air here pure as in the Montana mountains!
Sometime we must probe more deeply the problem of complicity.

Is civilization possible without it?

VISION

The vision will come—the Truth be revealed—but
Not even its vaguest nature you know—ah, truth

About what? But deep in the sibilant dark
That conviction irregularly

Gleams like fox-fire in sump-woods where,
In distance, lynx-scream or direful owl-stammer

Freezes the blood in a metaphysical shudder—which
Might be the first, feather-fine brush of Grace. Such

An event may come with night rain on roof, season changing
And bed too wide; or, say, when the past is de-fogged

And old foot tracks of folly show fleetingly clear before
Rationalization again descends, as from seaward.

Or when the shadow of pastness teasingly
Lifts and you recollect having caught—when, when?—

A glint of the nature of virtue like
The electrically exposed white of a flicker's

Rump feathers at the moment it flashes for the black thicket.
Or when, even, in a section of the city

Where no acquaintance would ever pass,
You watch snowflakes slash automobile lights

As you move toward the first
Illicit meeting, naturally at a crummy

Café. Your pace slows. You see her
Slip from the cab, dash for the door, dark fur coat
*

Collar up, head down. Inside,
As you order two highballs,

All eyes seem to focus on you. Drinks come, but
There is nothing to say. Hands

Do, damply, clasp—though no bed yet. Each stares
Into the other's eyes, desire like despair, and doom

Grows slow, and fat, and dark, like a burgundy begonia.
Soon you will watch the pale silken flash

Of well-turned ankles beneath dark fur,
As she hurries away on her stolen time, cab-hunting, and the future

Scarcely breathes. Your chest is a great clot. Perhaps then.
Oh, no. It may not happen, in fact, until

A black orderly, white-coated, on rubber soles, enters at 5 A.M.
The hospital room, suds and razor in hand, to shave,

With no word of greeting, the area the surgeon
Will penetrate. The robot departs. No one

Comes yet. Do not give up hope.
There is still time. Watch dawn blur the window.

Can it be that the vision has, long back, already come—
And you just didn't recognize it?

GLOBE OF GNEISS

How heavy is it? Fifteen tons? Thirty? More?—
The great globe of gneiss, poised, it would seem, by
A hair's weight, there on the granite ledge. Stop!
Don't go near! Or only on tiptoe. Don't,
For God's sake, be the fool I once was, who
Went up and pushed. Pushed with all strength,
Expecting the great globe to go
Hurtling like God's wrath to crush
Spruces and pines down the cliff, at least
Three hundred yards down to the black lake the last
Glacier to live in Vermont had left to await
Its monstrous plunge.

I pushed. It was like trying
To push a mountain. It
Had lived through so much, the incessant
Shove, like a shoulder, of north wind nightlong,
The ice-pry and lever beneath, the infinitesimal
Decay of ledge-edge. Suddenly,
I leaped back in terror.
Suppose!

So some days I now go again to see
Lichen creep slow up that
Round massiveness. It creeps
Like Time, and I sit and wonder how long
Since that gneiss, deep in earth,
In a mountain's womb, under
Unspeakable pressure, in total
Darkness, in unmeasurable
Heat, had been converted
From simple granite, striped now with something
Like glass, harder
Than steel, and I wonder
How long ago, and how, the glacier had found it.

How long and how it had trundled
The great chunk to globe-shape.

Then poised it on ledge-edge, in balanced perfection.

Sun sets. It is a long way
Down, the way darkening. I
Think how long my afternoon
Had seemed. How long
Will the night be?

But how short that time for the great globe
To remember so much!

How much will I remember tonight?

PART OF WHAT MIGHT HAVE BEEN A SHORT STORY, ALMOST FORGOTTEN

(octosyllabics)

Fifty-odd years ago if you
Were going to see Shoshone
Falls, the road was not, God knows, slicked
Up for the wheeled hordes of Nature-
Lovers gawking in flowered shirts
From Hawaii, and little bas-
tards strewing candy wrappers as
They come. No—rough roads then, gravel
Sometimes and, too, lonesomeness: no
Pervasive stink of burnt high-test,
Like the midnight memory of
Some act of shame long forgotten
But now back in sickening sweat.

The thunder, in vacant silence,
First grew like a dream of thunder,
Then external palpitation
Of air, not sound. Then, there it is—
The chasmed roar clambers now up
To smite you, as tons of water,
Glinting like steel, if steel could flow,
Plunge over geologic de-
bris to darkening depth where crash-
ing white and foam-stung air prove the
Great natural depth and shadow—
While the red sun of August, mis-
shapen, bloated, sinks to a far
Mountain heave.

The woman went back
To the car. Noise gave her headaches.

I watched the chasm darker grow,
And deeper while the white crashing
Momently seemed deeper, deeper,

But paradoxically loud-
er. I found myself drawn to the
Brink, gaze frozen downward. Arms, white,
Wreathed upward, imploring. I tore
My eyes from that compulsion, that
Deepening sound and white fulfill-
ment. I lifted eyes. Stared west. The
Sun, rim down now, flamed to the un-
winged, utmost, blank zenith of sky.
I stared till flame color, blood col-
or, faded to dusking color-
lessness, and the first star, westward
And high, spoke. Then, slowly, night. I
Heard the crash rise merciless, kept
Eyes on that first star. But sudden-
ly, glare of the car's headlights bursts.

Directly on me bursts. Then the
Scream. Then: "Look!" I turned to look and
There it was. On the slant of a
Skyward-broken stratum, among
Sparse scrub, it crouched, the great shoulder
Muscles bunched separate and high,
The noble head outthrust but mas-
sive jaws just clear of earth, upper
Lip drawn slightly back to expose
White glitter of fangs. The eyes, catch-
ing headlight glare, glared at me as
Vented from a skull with blown coals
Packed. The tail, in shadow, slow swung
From side to side. My blood was ice.

But no reason. With insolent,
Contemptuous dignity, its
Curiosity about this
Strange and defenseless beast now at
Last satisfied, it wheeled and took
One leap that, in slow grace, looked more
Like flight into blank darkness past
Lip of the chasm. That was all.
*

Back in my seat, the brake released,
I let the car coast out on the
Road such as it was. Turned switch. The
Motor snapped to life. My heart was
Slow again. We had seen what we
Had come to see, Nature's beauty,
But not what in the uncoiling
Of Time, Time being what it is,
We would come to see. Now under
White gaze in high darkness of in-
different stars, unknowing, word-
less, we lower swung, lower past
Tormented stone of crags, then in
Black maw of conifer forest:

And there, what beast might, waiting, be.

What beast with fang more white, with claw
More scimitar, with gaze of blaze
More metaphysical, patient
As stone in geological
Darkness, waits, waiting, will wait
Where and how long?—While we,
By other crag, by moonlit field,
By what star-tumbling stream, or through
What soundless snow which wipers groan
To cope with, roads poor-mapped, will move
Toward what foetal, fatal truth
Our hearts had witlessly concealed
In mere charade, hysterical

Or grave, of love.

COCKTAIL PARTY

Beyond the haze of alcohol and syntax and
Flung gage of the girl's glance, and personal ambition,
You catch some eye-gleam, sense a faint
Stir, as of a beast in shadow. It may be Truth.

Into what distance all gabble crawls away!
You look, and thirty lips move without sound
As though something had gone wrong with the TV,
And you see, of a sudden, a woman's unheard laugh exposing

Glitter of gold in the mouth's dark ghetto like unspeakable
Obscenity, but not sound. You try
To speak, an urgency like hard phlegm
In your throat, but no sound comes. You quiver, thinking

Of the horror of Truth. It lies in wait—ha, ha!—
A pun—or rises, diaphanous, like
Smoke from the red-stained cigarette butt
Half-crushed in a carved gold ashtray.

In wait, it lies. Or like a tumor grows
Somewhere inside your brain. Oh, doctor, please, oh,
Remove it! Expense be damned, I only
See lips moving. I move my lips, but no

Sound comes, not even a lie. Yes, operate, then I
Can hear them—and tell them I love them. At least,
If we are all to be victims of Truth,
Let us be destroyed together in normal communication.

Or maybe I'm only a little drunk. Oh, waiter!

DEEP—DEEPER DOWN

By five o'clock—still bright in spring—I'd catch
The first .44 explosion, cottony
In distance, but solid too, as though at the snatch
Of a ripe boll you'd found the hot slug inside, blood-wet. Then lonely

I'd shove back my afternoon chair, get old Luger, knee-boots,
And the German shepherd and pointer cross-breed that could smell
A cotton-mouth on a bridal wreath as well as on cypress roots,
And head for the bayou, now and then a yell.

For Jim, who'd cursed all day at a desk in town,
Was now free till dark, when his wife drove back.
So we wandered where water was black and slimy, or slickly brown,
And the bough with white blossoms was death—if it reared up its slack.

Two hours, perhaps, is enough to make a man feel
That reality spills into other hours to give
Life fundamental direction, and hand skill
To say, at his whim, *die* or *live*.

Jim and I took turns when a target presented itself.
If the first man missed, the second got two shots for his.
As I took aim I might often feel I was robbing his Self
Of its reason for being. I know what vanity is.

For spring and all summer that was our unspoken duty:
To purge earth of evil, and feel thereby justified.
In our wordless friendship we'd stare at the cleansing beauty
Of the dark arabesque wavering down, belly white as it died.

Long back, that was. Not to come again.
All gone—but dream once showed my own body glimmer down
Past the slick, slimy brush of a form that yet twisted in pain,
Its belly paling in darkness—deep—deeper down.

SKY

Livid to lurid switched the sky.
From west, from sunset, now the great dome
Arched eastward to lip the horizon edge,
There far, blank, pale. The grass, the trees,
Abandoned their kindly green to stretch
Into distance, arsenical now in that
Acid and arsenical light
Streaked yellow like urine.

Farmhouses afar—
They seemed to float, tiny and lost,
Swaying unmoored, forgotten in
That virulence past viridity
That washed, flooded, the world, and seemed
To lift all things, all houses, trees, hills,
From God-ordained foundations.

And
Your head in dizziness swam, while from
Southeast a blackness was towering
Toward you—sow-bellied, brute-nosed, coiling,
Twisting itself in pain, in rage,
And self-rage not yet discharged, and in
Its distant, sweeping downwardness
Uncentered pink flashes flickered pale but
In lethal promise. The sun's red eye
Now from western death glares.

We,
We all, have much endured, buckling
Belts, hearts. Have borne the outrageous
And uncomprehended inclemencies—
Borne even against God's will, or fate's.
Some have survived. We fear, yes. But

What most we fear advances on
Tiptoe, breath aromatic. It smiles.

Its true name is what we never know.

BETTER THAN COUNTING SHEEP

For a night when sleep eludes you, I have,
At last, found the formula. Try to summon

All those ever known who are dead now, and soon
It will seem they are there in your room, not chairs enough

For the party, or standing space even, the hall
Chock-full, and faces thrust to the pane to peer.

Then somehow the house, in a wink, isn't there,
But a field full of folk, and some,

Those near, touch your sleeve, so sadly and slow, and all
Want something of you, too timid to ask—and you don't

Know what. Yes, even in distance and dimness, hands
Are out—stretched to glow faintly

Like fox-fire in marshland where deadfall
Rots, though a few trunks unsteadily stand.

Meanwhile, in the grieving susurrus, all wordless,
You sense, at last, what they want. Each,

Male or female, young or age-gnawed, beloved or not—
Each wants to know if you remember a name.

But now you can't answer, not even your mother's name, and your heart
Howls with the loneliness of a wolf in

The depth of a snow-throttled forest when the moon, full,
Spills the spruce-shadows African black. Then you are, suddenly,

Alone. And your own name gone, as you plunge in ink-shadow or snowdrift.
The shadows are dreams—but of what? And the snowdrift, sleep.

THE CROSS

(A Theological Study)

Once, after storm, I stood at the cliff-head,
And up black basalt the sea's white claws
Still flung their eight fathoms to have my blood.
In the blaze of new sun they leap in cruel whiteness,
Not forgiving me that their screaming lunges
Had nightlong been no more than a dream
In the tangle and warmth and breathless dark
Of love's huddle and sleep, while stars were black
And the tempest swooped down to snatch our tiles.

By three, wind down and sun still high,
I walked the beach of the little cove
Where scavengings of the waves were flung—
Old oranges, cordage, a bottle of beer
With the cap still tight, a baby-doll
But the face smashed in, a boom from some mast,
And most desperately hunched by volcanic stone
As though trying to cling in some final hope,
But drowned hours back you could be damned sure,
The monkey, wide-eyed, bewildered yet
By the terrible screechings and jerks and bangs,
And no friend to come and just say *ciao*.

I took him up, looked in his eyes,
As orbed as dark aggies, as bright as tears,
With a glaucous glint in deep sightlessness,
Yet still seeming human with all they had seen—
Like yours or mine, if luck had run out.

So, like a fool, I said *ciao* to him.

Under wet fur I felt how skin slid loose
On the poor little bones, and the delicate
Fingers yet grasped, at God knew what.
So I sat with him there, watching wind abate.

No funnel on the horizon showed.
And of course, no sail. And the cliff's shadow
Had found the cove. Well, time to go.

I took time, yes, to bury him,
In a scraped-out hole, little cairn on top.
And I enough fool to improvise
A cross—

Two sticks tied together to prop in the sand.

But what use that? The sea comes back.

IV

TRUTH

Truth is what you cannot tell.
Truth is for the grave.
Truth is only the flowing shadow cast
By the wind-tossed elm
When sun is bright and grass well groomed.

Truth is the downy feather
You blow from your lips to shine in sunlight.

Truth is the trick that History,
Over and over again, plays on us.
Its shape is unclear in shadow or brightness,
And its utterance the whisper we strive to catch
Or the scream of a locomotive desperately
Blowing for the tragic crossing. Truth
Is the curse laid upon us in the Garden.

Truth is the Serpent's joke,

And is the sun-stung dust-devil that swirls
On the lee side of God when He drowses.

Truth is the long soliloquy
Of the dead all their long night.
Truth is what would be told by the dead
If they could hold conversation
With the living and thus fulfill obligation to us.

Their accumulated wisdom must be immense.

ON INTO THE NIGHT

On downward slope gigantic wheels
Of afternoon, how soundless crunch
Cloud cobbles of bright cumuli
Sparely paving the sky with white dreams of stone.

I lie beside the stream that slides
In the same windless silence beneath
Shadow of birch and beech and alder
Like an image of Time's metaphysic.

No insect hums. And taciturn,
The owl's adrowse in the depth of a cedar
To pre-enjoy the midnight's revel.
The thrush-throat only in silence throbs now.

Like film in silence being unspooled
From a defective mechanism,
The film of memory flows with no
Assessment of what it could ever mean.

Shadow and shade of cliff sift down
To darken the dimmest under-leaf,
And in the secret conduits
Of flesh I feel blood darker flow.

Now soon the evening's twitch begins
Beneath the prick of appetite
Or, nameless, of some instinctual tingle.
Bullbat and bat will soon scribble

Their lethal script on a golden sky.
From the apple orchard, a century ruined,
The he-bear will utter his sexual hoot,
Deer will come forth for autumn forage,
*

On the sleep-dazed partridge the lynx leaps
As the thrush-throat throbs to its last music.
Later, the last of night's voices is heard—
The owl's mystic question that follows his glut.

Then silence again. You sleep. Moonlight
Bathes the world in white silence. No, no!—there's one sound
Defined now by silence. The pump in your breast,
In merciless repetition, declares

Its task in undecipherable metaphor.

NO BIRD DOES CALL

Bowl-hollow of woodland, beech-bounded, beech-shrouded,
With roots of great gray boles crook'd airward, then down
To grapple again, like claws, in the breathless perimeter
Of moss, as in cave-shadow darker and deeper than velvet.

And even at noon just a flicker of light,
In summer green glint on darkness of green,
In autumn gold glint on a carpet of gold, for then
The hollow is Danae's lap lavished with gold by the god:

But what, through years now, I wake to remember
Is noontide of summer when, from sun-blast and world,
I, in despair, fled deeper and deeper,
To avoid the sight of mankind and the bustle of men,

And first, to that spot, came. No sound,
No movement of leaf, and I lay
In the hollow where moss was a soft depth like shadow.
With closed eyes I fell so slowly—so slow—as though

Into depth that was peace, but not death, and the world far away,
And one noon-ray strayed through labyrinths of leaves,
Revealing to me the redness of blood in eyelids,
And in that stillness my heart beat. The ray

Wandered on. The eyelids were darkened. I slept.
Then late, late, woke. Rose up. Wandered forth.
Came again where men were, and it seemed then that years—
How many?—had passed, and I looked back on life at great distance.

Years now have passed, and a thousand miles lie between,
And long since the time I would go there in every season
To stand in that silence, and hope for no bird, not any, to call.
And now when I wake in the night to remember, no bird ever calls.

WEATHER REPORT

In its deep little gorge my brook swells big,
The color of iron rust, and boulders bang—
Ah, where is the sun that yesterday made my heart glad?

Rain taps on the roof of my air-swung workhouse,
On one side in pine-tops above the gorge.
This the code now tapped: *Today is today.*

Where are the warblers that yesterday
Fluttered outside my screen walls, or ignoring
My presence, poured out their ignorant joy to my ignorant heart?

Where are the warblers? Why, yes, there's one,
Rain-colored like gunmetal now, rain-slick like old oil.
It is motionless in the old stoicism of Nature.

Yes, under a useless maple leaf,
The tail with a fringe of drops, like old Tiffany crystal,
And one drop, motionless, hangs at beak-tip.

I see that beak, unmoving as death—today
No note of ignorant joy to instruct
My ignorant heart, no promise of joy for tomorrow.

But the code yet taps on my tar-paper roof.
Have I read it aright? *Today is today.*
And earth grinds on, on its axis,

With a creak just this side of silence.
It lurches, perhaps.

TIRES ON WET ASPHALT AT NIGHT

As my head in darkness dents pillow, the last
Automobile, beyond rhododendrons
And evergreen screen, hisses
On rain-wet asphalt. It
Is going somewhere. I cannot
See it, but
It is going somewhere different
From here and now, leaving me
To lie and wonder what is left.

A man and a woman, perhaps they lean
Into cold dimness of gauge-lights, and she
At a flickering gap in my road-cover
Lifts head to catch glimpse of my bedroom windows
That glitter in darkness like
Two dead eyes that nobody has closed.

They do not know that I am here, eyes ceilingward,
Open to darkness. They do not know

That I am thinking of them—
How after the first shake and shudder at sheet-cold, they
Will huddle for warmth in the old
Mechanic hope of finding identity in
The very moment of paradox when
There is always none.

I stare into darkness ceilingward, thinking
How they at last must stare thus. And wonder
Do they, at least, clasp hands.

I think of the hiss of their tires going somewhere—
That sound like the *swish-hiss* of faint but continual
Wavelets far down on the handkerchief beach-patch
In a cove crag-locked and pathless, slotted

Only to seaward and westward, sun low. And I
Felt need to climb down and lie there, that sound
In my ear, and watch the sun sink, in its blaze, below
The blind, perpetual, abstract sea.

What then but climb again up, by stone-jut and scrub-root,
Hearing the loosened talus go tumbling down?
Once up, exhausted, face-down, arms outflung,
I lay clutching old clumps of summer-burned grass.
Was it fear that made me shake then? Or was I
Embracing the world?

It was a long way back home across darkening fields.

That was long ago. Till the hiss of the tires,
Like last wavelets, I had forgotten it.

I wish I could think what makes them come together now.

TIMELESS, TWINNED

Angelic, lonely, autochthonous, one white
Cloud lolls, unmoving, on an azure which
Is called the sky, and in gold drench of light,
No leaf, however gold, may stir, nor a single blade twitch,

Though autumn-honed, of the cattail by the pond. No voice
Speaks, since here no voice knows
The language in which a tongue might now rejoice.
So silence, a transparent flood, thus overflows.

In it, I drown, and from my depth my gaze
Yearns, faithful, toward that cloud's integrity,
As though I've now forgotten all other nights and days,
Anxiety born of the future's snare, or the nag of history.

What if, to my back, thin-shirted, brown grasses yet bring
The heat of summer, or beyond the perimeter northward, wind,
Snow-bellied, lurks? I stare at the cloud, white, motionless. I cling
To our single existence, timeless, twinned.

WHAT IS THE VOICE THAT SPEAKS?

What is the voice that speaks? Oh, tongue
Of laurel leaf by my glass door, trying

To tell how long since you lived on a mountain
In Tennessee, free wind inspiring your wisdom?

Or split tongue of *coluber constrictor*—
Black racer to you—who from his hole

In the lawn so valiantly rises to hiss at the cat, aggressive
And spread-clawed? Or the blind man who spat at you

When you put a dime in his cup at Christmas?
(Screw him, a dime is a dime, and suffering no index of virtue.)

Have you heard the great owl in the snow-pine? You know
His question—the one you've never, in anguish, been able to answer.

Yes, think of the wolf-howl, moonlit from mountain. How well
You remember, in warm bed, or season, from darkness that desolate timbre.

What did my mother, ready to die, say? "Son,
I like your new suit." Nor spoke again. Not to me.

And once, long distance, I heard a voice saying:
"I thought that you loved me—" And I:

"I do. But tomorrow's a snowflake in Hell."
And the phone went dead, and I thought of snow falling

All night, in white darkness, across the blindness of Kansas,
And wept, for I thought of a head thrown back, and the moan.

What tongue knows the name of Truth? Or Truth to come?
All we can do is strive to learn the cost of experience.

LANGUAGE BARRIER

Snow-glitter, snow-gleam, all snow-peaks
Scream joy to the sun. Green
Far below lies, shelved where a great *cirque* is blue, bluest
Of waters, face upward to sky-flaming blue. Then
The shelf falters, fails, and downward becomes

Torment and tangle of stone, like Hell frozen, where snow
Lingers only in shadow. Alone, alone,
What grandeur here speaks? The world
Is the language we cannot utter.
Is it a language we can even hear?

Years pass, and at night you may dream-wake
To that old altitude, breath thinning again to glory,
While the heart, like a trout,
Leaps. What,
Long ago, did the world try to say?

It is long till dawn.
The stars have changed position, a far train whistles
For crossing. Before the first twitter of birds
You may again drowse. Listen—we hear now
The creatures of gardens and lowlands.

It may be that God loves them, too.

LESSON IN HISTORY

How little does history manage to tell!
Did the lips of Judas go dry and cold on our Lord's cheek?

Or did tears unwittingly spring to his eyes
As lips found the flesh, torch-lit?

What song, in his screechy voice, and joy, did Boone
At sunset sing, alone in the wild Kentucky Eden?

Who would not envy Cambronne his famous obscenity—
At last, at last, fulfilling identity in pride?

Is it true that your friend was secretly happy when
The diagnostician admitted the growth was, in fact, malignant?

After mad Charlotte Corday had done her work,
Did she dip, trancelike, her hands in the water now staining the tub?

And what did Hendrik Hudson see
That last night, alone, as he stared at the Arctic sky?

Or what, at night, is the strange fulfillment, with anguish entwined,
As you wander the dark house, your wife not long dead?

What thought had Anne Boleyn as the blade, at last, rose?
Did her parts go moist before it fell?

And who will ever guess how you, night-waking,
See a corner of moonlit meadow, willows, sheen of the sibilant stream?

And know, or guess, what long ago happened there?
Or know what, in whisper, the water was trying to say?

PRAIRIE HARVEST

Look westward over forever miles of wheat stubble.
The roar of the red machines is gone, they are gone.
Their roar has left the heartbeat of silence. The bubble,
Enormous, red, molten, of sun, above the horizon,

Apparently motionless, hangs. Meanwhile, blue mist
For uncountable miles of the shaven earth's rondure arises,
And in last high light the bullbats gyre and twist,
Though in the world's emptiness the sound of their cries is

Nothing. Your heart is the only sound. The sun,
It is gone. Can it be that you, for an instant, forget
And blink your eyes as it goes? Another day done,
And the star the Kiowa once stared at will requite

Man's effort by lust, and lust by the lead-weighted eyes.
So you stand in the infinite circle, star after star,
And standing alone in starlight, can you devise
An adequate definition of self, whatever you are?

V

EAGLE DESCENDING

(To a dead friend)

Beyond the last flamed escarpment of mountain cloud
The eagle rides air currents, switch and swell,
With spiral upward now, steady as God's will.

Beyond black peak and flaming cloud, he yet
Stares at the sun—invisible to us,
Who downward sink. Beyond new ranges, shark-

Toothed, saw-toothed, he stares at the plains afar
By ghostly shadows eastward combed, and crossed
By a stream, steel-bright, that seems to have lost its way.

No silly pride of Icarus his! All peril past,
He westward gazes, and down, where the sun will brush
The farthermost bulge of earth. How soon? How soon

Will the tangent of his sight now intersect
The latitudinal curvature where the sun
Soon crucial contact makes, to leave him in twilight,

Alone in glory? The twilight fades. One wing
Dips, slow. He leans.—And with that slightest shift,
Spiral on spiral, mile on mile, uncoils

The wind to sing with joy of truth fulfilled.

BALLAD OF YOUR PUZZLEMENT

(How not to recognize yourself as what you think you are, when old and reviewing your life before death comes)

Purge soul for the guest awaited.
Let floor be swept, and let
The walls be well garlanded.

Put your lands and recollections
In order, before that hour,
For you, alas, are only

Recollections, but recollections
Like a movie film gone silent,
With a hero strange to you

And a plot you can't understand.
His face changes as you look.
He picks the scab of his heart.

He ponders, seems caught in the toils
Of ambiguous regrets,
Like a man with a passion for Truth

Who, clutching his balance-pole,
Looks down the sickening distance
On the crowd-swarm like ants, far below,

And he sways, high on the fated
And human high-wire of lies.
Does he feel the pitiless suction

Their eyes exert on him?
Does he know they wait the orgasmic
Gasp of relief as he falls?

Why doesn't he skyward gaze,
Then plunge—why doesn't he know
The true way to swap lies for Truth?
*

Then scene flicks to scene without nexus,
And to change the metaphor,
He sometimes seems like a fly

Stuck on the sweet flypaper
To struggle and strain to be free
Even as his senses reel

With the sweetness of deathly entrapment.
This puzzles you, but less than
The scene in the park woods,

Where the blade, flash-bright in darkness,
Slides slick to the woman's heart,
To the very hilt, and her mouth

Makes the shape of an *O* to make
The scream you can never hear.
She falls, and he bursts into tears.

Film blurs, goes black, but then
You see the hero kneeling,
Alone, alone, at prayer.

And later, after hiatus,
On a slum street, old now and stooped,
He meets the loathsome beggar

And stares at the sores and filth
With slow-rapt kinship. Draws
Out his last dollar bill, and thrusts

It into the claw-shaped hand—
Reaches out to touch the skin-cancer
That gnaws at a hideous cheek.

Then the flash to a country road
And fields stretching barren to distance.
He stands, gaze upward, then shakes
*

His fist at the height of sky.
But shrugs, and Chaplinesque,
Trudges on, alone, toward sunset.

Black goes the film, but blackness
Slashed by stab-jabs of white
That remind you of lightning bolts

At night, at a storm in the mountains—
But miniature, and no sound.
There is nothing left but silence

In which you hear your heart beat.
Yes, how many names has Truth?
Yes, how many lives have you lived?

Yes, all, all huddle together
In your Being's squirming nest,
Or perhaps you are only

A wind-dangled mirror's moment
That flickers in light-streaked darkness.
It is hard to choose your dream.

But at last, try to pull yourself
Together. Let floors be swept.
Let walls be well garlanded.

ANTINOMY: TIME AND IDENTITY

(1)

Alone, alone, I lie. The canoe
On blackness floats. It must
Be so, for up to a certain point
All comes back clear. I saw,
At dock, the canoe, aluminum, rising ghost-white on blackness.
This much is true. Silent,
As entering air, the paddle, slow, dips. Silent,
I slide forth. Forth on,
Forth into,
What new dimension? Slow
As a dream, no ripple at keel, I move through
The stillness, on blackness, past hope or despair
Not relevant now to illusion I'd once
Thought I lived by. At last,
Shores absorbed in the blackness of forest, I lie down. High,
Stars stare down, and I
See them. I wonder
If they see me. If they do, do they know
What they see?

(2)

Do I hear stars speak in a whisper as gentle as breath
To the few reflections caught pale in the blackness beneath?
How still is the night! It must be their voices.
Then strangely a loon-cry glows ember-red,
And the ember in darkness dims
To a tangle of senses beyond windless fact or logical choices,
While out of Time, Timelessness brims
Like oil on black water, to coil out and spread
On the time that seems past and the time that may come,
And both the same under
The present's darkening dome.

(3)

A dog, in the silence, is barking a county away.
It is long yet till day.

(4)

As consciousness outward seeps, the dark seeps in.
As the self dissolves, realization surrenders its burden
And thus fulfills your fictionality.
Night wind is no more than unrippling drift.
The canoe, light as breath, moves in a dignity
As soundless as a star's mathematical shift
Reflected light-years away
In the lake's black parodic sky.

I wonder if this is I.

(5)

It is not long till day.

(6)

Dawn bursts like the birth pangs of your, and the world's, existence.
The future creeps into the blueness of distance.
Far back, scraps of memory hang, rag-rotten, on a rusting barbed-wire fence.

(7)

One crow, caw lost in the sky-peak's lucent trance,
Will gleam, sun-purpled, in its magnificence.

TRIPS TO CALIFORNIA

Two days behind the dust-storm—man's
Fecklessness, God's wrath—and once
Dust on the highway piled so deep
Mules had to drag the car. This

Was Kansas, and in midafternoon
It rained blood for half an hour—
Or what looked red as blood, and what
Bible or folklore would call a rain

Of blood. It never rained any frogs,
Just blood. Then Garden City. What
A hell of a name! Dust heaped aside,
Faces stunned white. Eyes blank like those

Of people picked up in a lifeboat, the only
Survivors. "Whar goen?" This getting gas.
"Californ-ya, hanh? Not me. Out thar
Some day they'll git somethin wuss. I'll jist

Stick whar I knows whut the wust is."
On the road, west, a line of leafless
Black stubs of poplars—this now July—
Against the histrionic sunset.

The last ranch, dust windward to eaves.
Dead mule to lee, bloated like an
Enormous winter squash, green-blue.
This had been buffalo country, herds

Stretching for miles, parts of the two
Great herds, the South and the North, the mobile
Commissary for the Indians, but
The hunters took good care of that.
*

If you got a good "stand," Sharps rifles rang
All day, all night skinners working. Dawn
Then showed the hundred new naked corpses.
Besides, General Sheridan was a realist:

The only good one, he said, is a dead
One—not buffalo, but redskin.
Then plow, stupidity, avarice, did
The rest. But don't worry now. The tame

Continent eastward drops. Inferior
French wine for lunch. California
Waits like the dream it is, and mother
Of dreams. Reality past may be only

A dream, too. But, if so, sometimes
More naked, vivid, commanding than
Even anguish of immediacy,
For that comes piecemeal and guiltless from

Dark humus of history or our
Own fate, which blindly blooms, like a flower.

AUTO-DA-FÉ

Beautiful the intricacy of body!
Even when defective. But you have seen
Beauty beyond such watchmaker's craft,
For eyes unshutter in darkness to gleam out
As though to embrace you in holiness.

". . . though I give my body to be burned,
And have not . . ." You know the rest,
And how the "I" is not the "body."
At least, according to St. Paul's text.

Beautiful in whatever sense
The body be, it is but flesh,
And flesh is grass, the season short.
Is a bag of stercory, a bag
Of excrement, the worm's surfeit,
But a bag with movement, lusts, strange
Ecstasies, transports, and strange dreams.
But, oh!—not "I" but "body" screams
When flame licks like a lover. That
Is the pure language of body, purer
Than even the cry, ecstatic, torn out
At the crisis of body's entwinement. That voice
From flame has a glory wilder than joy
To resound forever in heart, mind,
And gut, with thrilled shock and soprano of Truth.

All history resounds with such
Utterance—and stench of meat burned:
Dresden and Tokyo, and screams
In the Wilderness as flame on the wounded
Encroached, and the soft-bellied citizen,
With swollen ego as he tests
The new Cadillac and, half-drunk, piles on-

to the goddam overpass buttress. Then flame.
You can be quite sure he screams. But

Some have not. Witches sometimes,
And saints and martyrs, no doubt in number.
Take Latimer or, evasion all past,
White-bearded Cranmer, who, in slow drizzle,
Outraces the pack, ragtag and bobtail—
Though old, first to the blessèd stake.
Climbs up. Waits. Composed, austere.
Faggots lighted, white beard prickling sudden in
Wisps of brightness, he into fire thrusts
The recreant hand. No, no, not his!—
That traitor in the house.

Or that
Cracked Maid, and her Voices that she, at the last,
Could not betray, though foreknowing the end.
Through dazzle and shimmer of flame-dance, she raptly
Fixed eyes on the tied-stick cross a brutish
Soldier held up. Her cry was a prayer.

Such evidence can scarcely attest
Sure meaning.

But executioners
Might choke flame to smoke to suffocate
Clients quickly. Or sometimes gunpowder in packets,
To belly affixed, made a human grenade
Timed short for the job. This, perhaps,
From some fumbling thought of the holiness or

Beauty of body.

ASPEN LEAF IN WINDLESS WORLD

Watch how the aspen leaf, pale and windless, waggles,
While one white cloud loiters, motionless, over Wyoming.
And think how delicately the heart may flutter
In the windless joy of unworded revelation.

Look how sea-foam, thin and white, makes its Arabic scrawl
On the unruffled sand of the beach's faint-tilted plane.
Is there a message there for you to decipher?
Or only the joy of its sunlit, intricate rhythm?

Is there a sign Truth gives that we recognize?
Can we fix our eyes on the flight of birds for answer?
Can the bloody-armed augurs declare expediency?
What does dew on stretched wool-fleece, the grass dry, mean?

Have you stood on the night-lawn, oaks black, and heard,
From bough-crotch to bough-crotch, the moon-eyed tree-toad utter,
Again and again, that quavery croak, and asked
If it means there'll be rain? Toward dawn? Or early tomorrow?

We were not by when Aaron laid down his rod
That suddenly twisted, went scaly, and heaved the fanged head,
And when Egypt's high magi probed their own lore for the trick—
Well, the sacred serpent devoured that brood. What, now,

Would you make of that? Yes, we wander our shadowy world
Of miracles, whispers, high jinks, and metaphor.
Yes, why is the wind in the cedar the sub-sob of grief?
And the puppy—why is his tongue on your palm so sweet?

What image—behind blind eyes when the nurse steps back—
Will loom at the end of your own life's long sorites?
Would a sun then rise red on an eastern horizon of waters?
Would you see a face? What face? Would it smile? Can you say?
*

Or would it be some great, sky-thrusting gray menhir?
Or what, in your long-lost childhood, one morning you saw—
Tinfoil wrappers of chocolate, popcorn, nut shells, and poorly
Cleared up, the last elephant turd on the lot where the circus had been?

ACQUAINTANCE WITH TIME IN EARLY AUTUMN

Never—yes, never—before these months just passed
Had I known the nature of Time, and felt its strong heart,
Stroke by stroke, against my own, like love,
But love without face, or shape, or history—
Pure Being that, by being, our being denies.

Summer fulfills the field, the heart, the womb,
While summerlong, infinitesimally,
Leaf stem, at bough-juncture, dries,
Even as our tireless bodies plunge,
With delicious muscular flexion and heart's hilarity,
White to the black ammoniac purity of
A mountain pool. But black
Is blue as it stares up at summer's depthless azure,
And azure was what we saw beneath
At the timeless instant hanging
At arc-height.

Voices of joy how distant seem!
I float, pubic hair awash, and gaze
At one lone leaf, flame-red—the first—alone
Above summer's bulge of green,
High-hung against the sky.

Yes, sky was blue, but water, I suddenly felt,
Was black, and striped with cold, and one cold claw
Reached ghostly up
To find my flesh, to pierce
The heart, as though
Releasing, in that dark inwardness,
A single drop. Oh, leaf,

Cling on! For I have felt knee creak on stair,
And sometimes, dancing, notice how rarely

A girl's inner thigh will brush my own,
Like a dream. Whose dream?

The sun
Pours down on the leaf its lacquer of Chinese red.

Then, in the lucent emptiness,
While cries of joy of companions fade,
I feel that I see, even in
The golden paradox of air unmoving
Each tendon of that stem, by its own will,
Release
Its tiny claw-hooks, and trust
A shining destiny. The leaf—it is
Too moorless not to fall. But
Does not. Minutely,
It slides—calm, calm—along the air sidewise,
Sustained by the kiss of under-air.

While ages pass, I watch the red-gold leaf,
Sunlit, descend to water I know is black.
It touches. Breath
Comes back, and I hate God
As much as gravity or the great globe's tilt.

How shall we know the astrolabe of joy?
Shall gratitude run forward as well as back?
Who once would have thought that the heart,
Still ravening on the world's provocation and beauty, might,
After time long lost
In the tangled briars of youth,
Have picked today as payday, the payment

In life's dime-thin, thumb-worn, two-sided, two-faced coin?

SAFE IN SHADE

Eyes, not bleared but blue,
Of the old man, horizonward gazed—
As on horizons and years, long lost, but now
Projected from storage in that capacious skull.

He sat in his big chair propped
Against reddish tatter of
Bole-bark of the great cedar. I,
The boy who on the ground sat, waited.

I waited for him to speak.

I waited for him to come back to me
From the distances he traveled in.
I waited for him to speak. I saw
The cob pipe in the liver-spotted hand
Now propped on a knee, on the washed blue-jeans.
Smoke, frail, slow, blue—as blue
As the jeans but not the eyes—
Rose to thread the cedar-dark.

Around us in our shade and hush
Roared summer's fierce fecundity,
And the sun struck down,
In blare and dazzle, on the myth of the world, but we
Safe in the bourne of distance and shade,
Sat so silent that, from woods coming down
To the whitewashed fence but yards behind me,
I heard the secret murmur and hum
That in earth, on leaf, in air, seethed. Heard
One jay, outraged, scream.
The old blue eyes, they fixed on me.

I waited for him to speak. He spoke.
*

Into the world hurled,
In later times and other places,
I lived but as man must
In all the garbled world's compulsions,
By fate perforce performed
Acts evil or good, or even
Both in the same gesture, in
That paradox the world exemplifies.

And Time, like wind-tattered smoke,
Blew by for one who, like all men, had flung,
In joy and man's maniacal
Rage, his blood
And the blind, egotistical, self-defining
Sperm into
That all-devouring, funnel-shaped, mad and high-spiraling,
Dark suction that
We have, as the Future, named.

Where is my cedar tree?

Where is the Truth—oh, unambiguous—
Thereof?

SYNONYMS

(1)

Where eons back, earth slipped and cracked
To leave a great stratum, snag-edged, thrust

As margin to that blind inwardness, water
Now plunges in cosmic racket, sempiternal roar,

White-splintered on masses of stone, deep-domed or spired,
Chaos of white in dark paradox. What is the roar

But a paradox in that
Tumultuous silence—

Which paradox must be a voice of ultimate utterance?

(2)

When the last thrush knows the hour past song
Has come, the westward height yet
Stays sallow, and bats scribble
The sky in minuscule murder, which,
From one perspective, is beauty, too.
Time will slip in silence past, like God's breath.

Who will see the first star tonight above the mountain?

(3)

Lean back, one hand on saddle-horn, if you must.
Watch stones and gravel slip and cascade
Down each side of the knife-edge trail.
Just trust your mountain-mount and God,
For there is an end to human judgment.
Unless you stay at home in bed. Look!
Miles west, far down, a river
Crawls, like a blue snake,
Toward Wyoming.

To one side,
On a stunt stub of pine, only one
Raw spray of green visible, a magpie,
Wag-tailed in wind, sits, and with eyes
Like shiny, old-fashioned
Shoe-buttons, observes you.

He has been waiting for something
Funny and disastrous to happen.

(4)

Have you—scarcely more than a boy—been
The last man afield, the old binder
Dragged off, sun low? Have you stood
Among shadowy wheat shocks, the tips
Of stalks showing gold in that last light? Beyond
Shorn earth the sun sags slow red. In distance
One cowbell spills
The empty tinkle of loneliness. A bullfrog,
Brass-bellied, full-throated,
Accents the last silence.

Long later the owl.

Your hands still ache from the pitchfork heft.

Why do you, young, feel tears in your eyes?

(5)

Riding in riot and roil of Aegean blue and gold light,
Eastward broad reaching, wind
Northwesterly, force 6, gusting 7, seas smacking
Her quarter, the big yawl, hard-driven,
Thrusts merciless forefoot
Through tasseled silk-swell to swing
Scuppers under, then lifting, wet-waisted, sun-bright. Under
My desperate handgrip the cap-shroud
Strains in joy of its strength and musical hum.

Wind tears at my oilskins, spume
Burns eyeballs, but I can yet see
White flash of glitters blown down the sky
Till one, on a pivot of wing-tip, Nijinski-like, swings
To a motionless, lateral joy, beak north,
While the world, far below, and its tumult fulfill
The mission of mythic and beautiful rage.
In which each of us, a particle, partakes
Of its microscopic part.

Wind down, tonight shall we moor
In a crag-locked bay without
One wavelet to lap the sixty-foot hull,
And wordless, there being no moon, stare up
At the astute complex
Of enormous, white, and foreign stars?

What other eyes have stared there before?

(6)

In the narrow, decrepit old street where day-gleam
Is throttled as tenements shoulder each other for mutual support,
Cab, car, and truck scream
In anguish and anger for space, and fumes burn the eyes,
And swirl, sweat, stink, and foreign tongues abort
Whatever seems human, and nothing human replies.
This, the swelter of summer: at evening on stair,
Street step, cellar step, the old and the sick gasp for air,
And at night, then muggings and rape become sport.

Morning: arrange the principals, for soon—
Action! A middle-aged drunk sits and sways
On curbstone, bottle in hand, tweeds from better days.
Takes a long pull, sags flat, seems fixed till afternoon,
And a grubby old dame, one hand on a cane,
The other, to let down her hulk and sore foot with less pain,
Clutches the iron rail of the old stone
Street-steps. Descends. The great garbage grinder
Screams at its task, but a cab, breaking through,
Flings a kitten aside among filth, where san-men will find her.

But she scrambles out, one leg broken, or two,
To curbside. The boss of the monster, quick as a wink,
Seizes tail, swings her high, choking with laughter to think
How she tries to climb air with mangled, or unmangled, paws.
Still laughing, he holds up the creature so all may look
And relish the joke, but blinded by mirth,
He doesn't see the old dame swing her cane, and the crook
Yanks down his wrist, and despite sore foot, bulk, and girth,
She thrusts the poor prize in the improvised sack of her apron, gives
A long wheeze, and painfully climbs up where she lives.

There's enough laughing now, and the boss flees the public eye.
The drunk staggers up, hiccups, hitches pants,
Takes swig, lifts a half-empty quart to the sky,
And in the rapt voice of a prophet makes utterance:
"Lord God, can't You see the hour to smite!—
Or lost Your nerve, huh? Can't longer tell wrong from right?"
*

And a little stall-keeper creeps back to his hole in the wall,
Where vegetables, sprinkled, look nigh as fresh as they grow.
Yet one by one, he surveys the condition of all.
Then with edge of his apron, he buffs an apple to glow.

And another. Another. Blind impulse had prompted
The act. —Just what, he could not know.

(7)

There are many things in the world, and I have seen some.
Some things in the world are beautiful, and I
Have seen some. But more things are to come,
And in the world's tangled variety,
It is hard sometimes to remember that beauty is one word for reality.

SWIMMING IN THE PACIFIC

At sunset my foot outreached the mounting Pacific's
Last swirl as tide climbed, and I stood
On the mile-empty beach backed by dune-lands. Turned, saw,
Beyond knotting fog-clots, how Chinaward now
The sun, a dirty pink smudge, grew larger, smokier,
More flattened, then sank.

Through sand yet sun-hot, I made to my landmark—
Gray cairn to guard duck pants (not white now), old drawers,
Old sneakers, T-shirt, my wallet (no treasure).
At dune-foot I dressed,
Eyes westward, sea graying, one gull at
Great height, but not white-bright, the last
Smudge of sun being gone.

So I stood, and I thought how my years, a thin trickle
Of sand grains—years I then could
Count on few as fingers and toes—had led me
Again and again to this lonesome spot where
The sea might, in mania, howl, or calm, lure me out
Till the dunes were profiled in a cloud-pale line,
Nothing more,
Though the westering sun lured me on.

But beachward by dusk, drawn back
By the suction of years yet to come—
So dressed now, I wandered the sand, drifting on
Toward lights, now new, of the city afar, and pondered
The vague name of Time,
That trickles like sand through fingers,
And is life.

But suppose, after sorrow and joy, after all
Love and hate, excitement and roaming, failure, success,
And years that had long trickled past

And now could certainly never
Be counted on fingers and toes—suppose
I should rise from the sea as of old
In my twilit nakedness,
Find my cairn, find my clothes, and in gathering fog,
Move toward the lights of the city of men,
What answer, at last,
Could I give my old question? Unless,
When the fog closed in,
I simply lay down, on the sand supine, and up
Into grayness stared and, staring,

Could see your face, slow, take shape.

Like a dream all years had moved to.

NIGHT WALKING

Bear, my first thought at waking. I hear
What I think is the first bear this year
Come down off the mountain to rip
Apples from trees near my window—but no,
It's the creak of the door of the shop my son stays in.
Now booted and breeched but bare
From waist, he now stands
Motionless, silent, face up
To the moon, tonight full, now late and zenithward high
Over forests as black as old blood
And the crags bone-white.

My Levis now on, and boots, I wait.
For what? I creep
Behind a parked car and guiltily crouch.

His face, brown but now talc-white in moonlight,
Lifts moonward, and I remember how once,
Footloose in Greece, in the mountains, alone, asleep,
He had waked, he said, at a distant dog's howl and
Stood up in a land where all is true.

I crouch as he slowly walks up the track
Where from blackness of spruces great birches
Stand monitory, stand white—
Moving upward, and on, face upward as though
By stars in an old sea he steered.

In silence and shadow and in
The undefinable impulse to steal
What knowledge I, in love, can,
With laggard cunning I trail to the first ridge-crest.
He stops. His gaze
Turns slow, and slower,
From quarter to quarter, over

The light-laved land, over all
Thence visible, river and mowings,
Ruined orchards, ledges and rock-slides,
And the clambering forest that would claim all.

Last, the next range to westward.

High, calm, there the moon rides.
He lifts up his light-bleached arms.
He stands.

Arms down, goes on.

I do not guess
How far he will go, but in my
Mixture of shame, guilt, and joy do know
All else is his—and alone.

In shadow, I huddle
Till I can start back to bed and the proper darkness of night.

I start, but alone then in moonlight, I stop
As one paralyzed at a sudden black brink opening up,
For a recollection, as sudden, has come from long back—
Moon-walking on sea-cliffs, once I
Had dreamed to a wisdom I almost could name.
But could not. I waited.
But heard no voice in the heart.
Just the hum of the wires.

But that is my luck. Not yours.

At any rate, you must swear never,
Not even in secret, the utmost, to be ashamed
To have lifted bare arms to that icy
Blaze and redeeming white light of the world.

PASSERS-BY ON SNOWY NIGHT

Black the coniferous darkness,
White the snow track between,
And the moon, skull-white in its starkness,
Watches upper ledges lean,

And regards with the same distant stare,
And equal indifference,
How your breath goes white in steel air
As you trudge to whither *from* whence.

For from somewhere you rose to go,
Maybe long before daylight withdrew,
With the dream of a windowpane's glow
And a path trodden to invite you.

And, indeed, there may be such place,
Perhaps at next corner or swerve,
Where someone presses a face
To the frost-starred glass, though the curve

Shows yet only mocking moonlight.
But soon, but soon!—Alone,
I wish you well in your night
As I pass you in my own.

We each hear the distant friction,
Then crack of bough burdened with snow,
And each takes the owl's benediction,
And each goes the way he will go.

AFTERTHOUGHT

The less a poet says about his poems, perhaps the better, but I hazard an afterthought. Upon finishing this book, a reader may feel that a few poems are, in both feeling and style, off the main impulse—accidents, sports, irrelevances; but they are not accidents or sports, and I hope not, in the last analysis, irrelevances.

Rather early, as the book began to take shape in my mind and in some poems, I began to feel that I needed a preliminary poem and another as a sort of coda, both very simple in method and feeling, to serve as a base for the book, or better, as a bracket to enclose the dimly envisaged tangles and complications of the main body. So "October Picnic Long Ago" and "Passers-by on Snowy Night" were composed well before the book had begun to assume anything like its final content and structure.

I may also mention "Empty White Blotch on Map of Universe: a Possible View" and "Ballad of Your Puzzlement," both of which are rather like sore thumbs, at least at first glance. It might be said that both, if taken in isolation, may well be seen not only as peculiar in style, but as having meanings quite contradictory to the tone and intent of the work as a whole. Here, however, it should be remembered that the first, as the title indicates, is only "a Possible View"—a parodic and disintegrating account of the history of man's striving for spiritual values and a sense of community, with only a defeated and pathetic romantic sexual yearning left in the end. This is intended to serve as an introduction to a section chiefly concerned with the issues ironically raised in the poem. It is concerned to serve as a kind of backboard against which the poems of the section are bounced. As for "The Ballad of Your Puzzlement," it has a parenthetic subtitle which is suppose to indicate that this poem, like the other just discussed, may also serve ironically as a backboard for the concluding section. This section is, of course, concerned with the reviewing of life from the standpoint of age. But this is not the place for an attempt at explication. Nor is this the proper author for such explication.

There is one more thing I may mention. The order of the poems is not the order of composition (and certain poems composed during the general period are not included). The order and selection are determined thematically, but with echoes, repetitions, and variations in feeling and tonality. Here, as in life, meaning is, I should say, often more fruitfully found in the question asked than in any answer given. The thematic order—or better, structure—is played against, or with, a shadowy narrative, a shadowy autobiography, if you will. But this is an autobiography which represents a fusion of fiction and fact in varying degrees and perspectives. As with question and answer, fiction may often be more deeply significant than fact. Indeed, it may be said that our lives are our own supreme fiction.

ABOUT THE AUTHOR

ROBERT PENN WARREN was born in Guthrie, Kentucky, in 1905. After graduating summa cum laude from Vanderbilt University (1925), he received a master's degree from the University of California (1927) and did graduate work at Yale University (1927–28) and at Oxford as a Rhodes Scholar (B.Litt., 1930).

Mr. Warren has published many books, including ten novels, thirteen volumes of poetry, and a volume of short stories; also, a play, a collection of critical essays, a biography, two historical essays, a critical book on Dreiser and a study of Melville, and two studies of race relations in America. This body of work has been published in a period of fifty years—a period during which Mr. Warren has also had an active career as a professor of English.

All the King's Men (1946) was awarded the Pulitzer Prize for Fiction. The Shelley Memorial Award recognized Mr. Warren's early poetry. *Promises* (1957) won the Pulitzer Prize for Poetry, the Edna St. Vincent Millay Prize of the Poetry Society of America, and the National Book Award. In 1944–45 Mr. Warren was the second occupant of the Chair of Poetry at the Library of Congress. In 1952 he was elected to the American Philosophical Society; in 1959 to the American Academy of Arts and Letters; and in 1975 to the American Academy of Arts and Sciences. In 1967 he received the Bollingen Prize in Poetry for *Selected Poems: New and Old, 1923–1966,* and in 1970 the National Medal for Literature and the Van Wyck Brooks Award for the book-length poem *Audubon: A Vision.* In 1974 he was chosen by the National Endowment for the Humanities to deliver the third Annual Jefferson Lecture in the Humanities. In 1975 he received the Emerson-Thoreau Award of the American Academy of Arts and Sciences. In 1976 he received the Copernicus Award from the Academy of American Poets, in recognition of his career but with special notice of *Or Else—Poem/Poems 1968–1974.* In 1977 he received the Harriet Monroe Prize for Poetry. He is a Chancellor of the Academy of American Poets. In 1979, for *Now and Then,* a book of poems, he received his third Pulitzer Prize.

Mr. Warren lives in Connecticut with his wife, Eleanor Clark (author of *Rome and a Villa, The Oysters of Locmariaquer, Baldur's Gate, Eyes, Etc.: A Memoir,* and *Gloria Mundi*). They have two children, Rosanna and Gabriel.